Science 3B

Joe
Sue
Zoe

Written by:

Teo-Gwan Wai Lan • Dr Kwa Siew Hwa • Koh Siew Luan • Renee Chong

General Editor:

Dr Lee Sing Kong

FEDERAL PUBLICATIONS

An imprint of Times Media

Preface

My Pals are Here! **Science** is a comprehensive Primary Science programme based on the latest guidelines set by the Ministry of Education. In this series, Science is viewed as a fascinating subject that attempts to answer questions about the world around us. This is accomplished through the plentiful use of colourful photographs and amusing illustrations. The subject is taught through inquiry and investigation, and pupils are encouraged to be actively involved in seeking answers to problems. All these aim to enhance learning and impress upon pupils that Science is all around them.

My Pals are Here! **Science** adopts a thematic approach. The four themes covered in Primary 3 are **Diversity**, **Cycles**, **Systems** and **Interactions**. Where possible, relationships between the topics in each theme are demonstrated. This enables pupils to appreciate links between seemingly different topics, and to connect scientific ideas.

My Pals are Here! **Science** has infused the initiatives of thinking skills, national education and the use of information technology into the teaching of Science. Each level of the programme consists of a Textbook, an Activity Book, a Workbook and a Teacher-assist Pack.

Group & Share

Thought-provoking questions to stimulate thinking and discussion

Bits 'n' Bites

Check out interesting bits of information related to the topic

To make the study of Science more interesting, the following features have been included:

Mammals are the only animals with hair on their bodies. They are also the only animals that feed their babies the mother's milk.

Babies feeding on the mother's milk

birth to their young. Two mammals which lay are the spiny anteater platypus.

platypus

Birds

Birds are easily identified by the feathers on their bodies. They are the only animals with feathers.

All birds have a beak, two wings and two legs.

45

Some animals give birth to their young. The young grow fully inside the bodies of these animals before they are born. Animals such as cows, giraffes and whales give birth to their young.

Animals can be different in many ways. This is what makes them so fascinating. Perhaps this explains why the Singapore Zoological Gardens is one of the most popular attractions in Singapore!

At a glance...
- All animals eat other living things for food.
- Animals are different in many ways. They
  - are of different sizes, shapes and colours
  - live in different places
  - move in different ways
  - have different outer coverings
  - eat different kinds of food
  - reproduce in different ways

Cool to Do

1 Find out which animal on land is the largest and which animal in the sea is the largest.
2 Some animals are becoming extinct because humans hunt them for their outer coverings. Find out what some of these animals are. Here are some websites you may like to visit:

http://www.defenders.org/kidsplanet/
http://www.vegan.com/current/fur.html
http://www.clci.mb.ca/mmedia/Endangered.htm

You may also use the key phrase 'endangered AND fur' to search for other websites.
3 Cut out pictures of animals from magazines or newspapers. Try grouping them in different ways, for example, according to where they live, the food they eat, or their outer coverings.

41

At a glance...
Gives an overall view of the topic

Cool to Do

Fun extension activities to encourage independent exploration beyond curriculum time. Activities include those that involve research or require the use of computers.

Acknowledgements

The publisher wishes to thank the following organisations and individuals for granting permission to reproduce the images and poem listed.

Photo Credits
Cliff B. Frith/Bruce Coleman Inc.: p14 (TL)
Lee Sing Kong: pp 17 (C, BR), 18 (TC, BC) and 19 (TL, TR)
Natsteel Ltd: p84 (BL)
Nicholas Birks/Auscape: p25 (CL)
Singapore Zoological Gardens: pp 6 (CR), 7 (T, B), 13 (TR, BR) and 14 (B)
Tan Heok Hui: p25 (TR)
Vision Photo Agency Pte Ltd: p25 (BL)
Wee Yeow Chin: pp 10 (CL, BL), 11 (T, BR) and 12 (TL, B)

Text Acknowledgement
Poem from LIFE EDUCATION: MY WONDERFUL BODY first published in the
UK by Franklin Watts, a division of the Watts Publishing Group Limited,
96 Leonard Street, London EC2A 4XD: p49

The publisher is also grateful to the following organisation and individuals.

- Noble International Pte Ltd for sponsoring some of the objects used in this book: pp 67 (ring and button magnets), 70 (horseshoe magnets), 74 (ring magnets) and 83 (magnetic noticeboard)

- Models Amil, Douglas, Genevieve, Rena and their families

- All those who have kindly loaned the publisher items for the photos featured

Contents

THEME 2 : Cycles

THEME 3 : Systems

THEME 4 : Interactions 64

Cycles

Can you solve this puzzle?

How do you know which shape to place in the space?

If you look at the shapes before the space, you will notice that there is a pattern. This pattern, repeats itself. It can go on and on, but you will need lots and lots of paper and time to draw the repeating shapes.

Here is a way of showing such a pattern.

A pattern that repeats itself again and again is called a **cycle**. You can tell what comes next in a cycle.

A day is made up of morning, afternoon and night. This happens every day in the same pattern. After night comes morning and so begins another day. Morning, afternoon and night form a cycle.

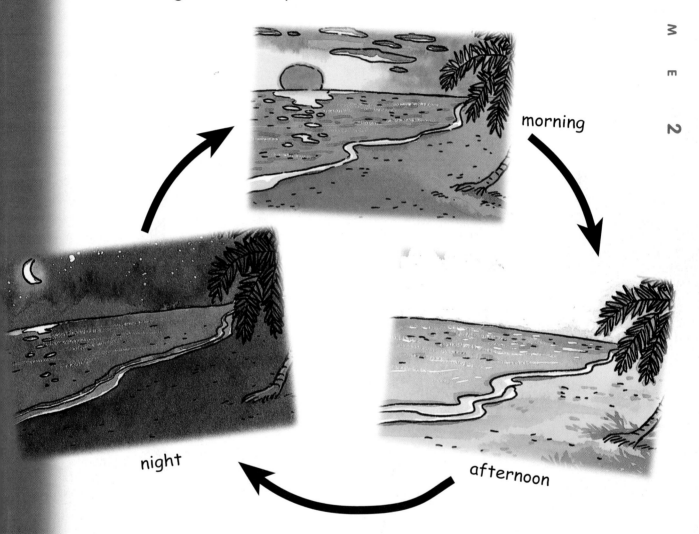

morning

afternoon

night

Some cycles take a short time to complete, while others take a long time. The change from morning to afternoon, then to night takes a day. However, the change in seasons, from spring to summer, autumn, then to winter, takes a year.

Do you know of some things around you that happen in cycles?

9 Life Cycles

Hmm... I see a pattern. Eggs hatch into chicks. The chicks will grow into adult chickens and then the hens will lay eggs. Hey! I can see a cycle in the life of a chicken!

What is a Life Cycle?

All living things go through a cycle called a **life cycle**. Living things are hatched or born, they grow bigger and older, before they finally die. If they reproduce while they are alive, the cycle repeats itself. The young go through a similar life cycle as the parents. In this way, living things of the same kind continue to be found on Earth.

egg

chick

adult chicken

You have seen that a chicken egg hatches into a chick, and a chick grows into an adult chicken. These are the **stages** of growth in the life cycle of a chicken.

3

Different living things pass through different stages of growth before they become adults. Some pass through more stages. Others pass through fewer stages. Some look very much the same at the various stages. Some look very different. For example, the beetle looks so different at the various stages of growth that it is hard to believe that the young and the adult are actually the same kind of living thing!

The beetle looks very different at the different stages of growth.

Some life cycles are short. Others are very long. Fruit flies have very short life cycles. After the young hatch from the eggs, they grow into adults and die within a few weeks. Some trees, on the other hand, have life cycles lasting for several hundred years!

At a glance...

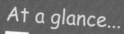 A pattern that repeats itself over and over again is a cycle.

Every living thing goes through a life cycle. It is hatched or born. It grows into an adult before it finally dies.

A life cycle is made up of a number of stages of growth.

Life Cycles of Some Animals

Life Cycle of a Chicken

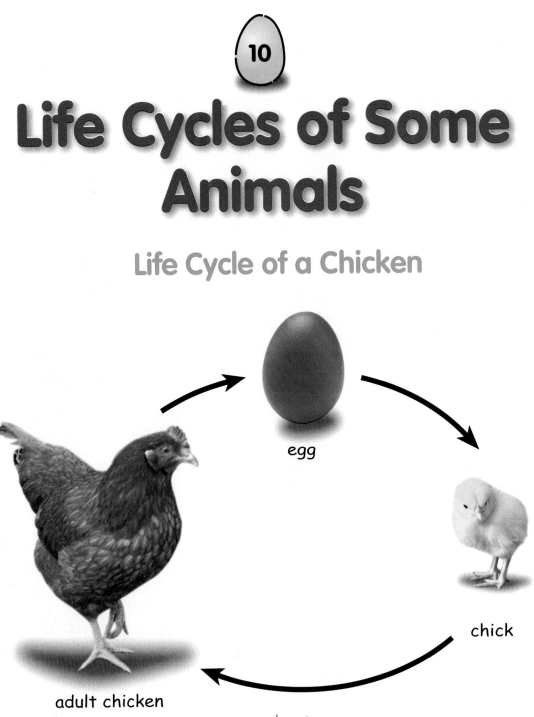

egg

chick

adult chicken

Life cycle of a chicken

Bits 'n' Bites

An incubator is a machine that can do the job of a hen in hatching eggs.

The life of a chicken starts as an egg. After the eggs are laid, the hen usually sits on them. Do you know why?

During this time, you do not see anything happening from the outside of the egg. However, many activities are taking place inside it. The chick is developing very quickly.

These changes happen within 21 days.

About 21 days after the egg is laid, it hatches into a chick.

A chick pecks at the eggshell to crack it so that it can come out of the egg.

A chick looks like its parents in many ways. As it grows, it becomes even more like its parents. One day, it will be able to reproduce and a new life cycle starts.

Like the chick, many baby animals look like their parents. They are just smaller in size than the adults. Hence it is quite easy to match the young with their parents.

Can you match the babies with their parents?

However, there are some baby animals that look very different from their parents! Can you name any of them?

9

Life Cycles of Insects

The life cycles of some insects are exciting to watch. These insects pass through stages of growth where they look nothing like their parents. As they grow, they change from one form into another.

Life cycle of a butterfly

When a female butterfly is ready to lay its eggs, it flies around to find the right plant. It needs to lay its eggs on a suitable plant so that her young will have food. Once the butterfly finds the right plant, it lays its eggs on the leaves or the stem. Then it flies off and leaves the eggs to hatch on their own.

Each egg hatches into a **larva**. The larva is the young of an insect. The larva of a butterfly has a special name. It is called a **caterpillar**. A caterpillar looks like a tiny wriggly worm and is very different from the adult butterfly.

Caterpillars hatching from eggs

Do not be fooled by the caterpillar's small size. It has a huge appetite! All it does is eat and grow. It never moves far from the plant that gives it food.

A caterpillar is often called an eating machine because all it does is eat to prepare itself for the next stage!

The caterpillar grows very fast. In just a few days, it is too big for its skin. It grows a new skin and sheds the old one. This is called **moulting**. The caterpillar moults several times as it grows bigger and bigger.

Soon it is about time for the caterpillar to enter the next stage of the life cycle. It starts to move more slowly. It stops feeding. Then it fastens itself to a leaf or twig and spins a case around itself.

Case formed by a caterpillar

The caterpillar has now changed into a **pupa**. The pupa may look inactive on the outside, but inside, amazing changes are taking place.

When the case finally breaks open, a beautiful butterfly comes out of it. The butterfly spreads its wings to dry. Then it takes off on its first flight.

The butterfly flies from plant to plant to feed on the nectar of flowers. When the right time arrives, the female butterfly may also lay eggs and a new life cycle starts.

Bits 'n' Bites

Most butterflies live for less than three weeks.

The life cycle of the butterfly has four stages. Each stage looks very different from another.

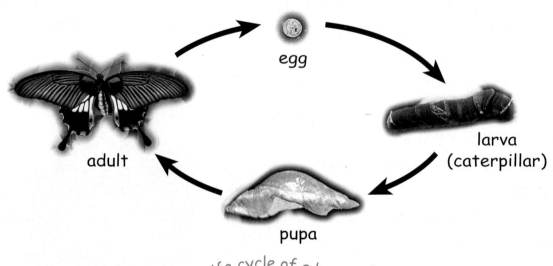

egg

larva (caterpillar)

pupa

adult

Life cycle of a butterfly

Life cycle of a cockroach

This is not a seed. It is actually an egg case of a cockroach.

A female cockroach lays its eggs in an egg case. It then leaves the egg case in a dark, safe place. Each egg case may contain 16 to 50 eggs, depending on the type of cockroach. The eggs are left to hatch on their own.

Group & Share

How does the dark brown colour of the egg case help to protect it?

Each egg hatches into a small young cockroach. A young cockroach is called a **nymph**. It looks very much like the adult, but it is smaller and does not have wings. A nymph runs around and eats a great deal. It is not a fussy eater and feeds on anything it can find. This includes leftover food, paper, clothing, and even dirt.

13

As the nymph grows bigger, its body soon becomes too big for the hard body covering. It moults. The nymph continues to grow and it moults several more times before it becomes an adult.

An adult cockroach has wings. It may live for several months to over a year. If it reproduces during this time, a new life cycle starts.

Nymph moulting

You have seen that the life cycle of a cockroach has three stages. They are:

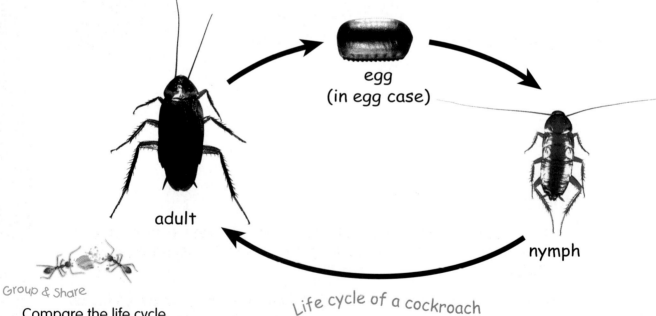

adult

egg
(in egg case)

nymph

Life cycle of a cockroach

Group & Share

Compare the life cycle of a cockroach to that of a butterfly. How are they different?

At a glance...

☐ A chicken passes through these stages in its life cycle:

egg → chick → adult chicken → egg

☐ A butterfly passes through these stages in its life cycle:

egg → larva → pupa → adult butterfly → egg

☐ A cockroach passes through these stages in its life cycle:

egg → nymph → adult cockroach → egg

Cool to Do

1 Find out about the life cycles of other animals by visiting the library or websites on the internet, or by talking to pet owners or people who look after animals.

2 Look for frog eggs in drains or ponds. When you do this, make sure you are accompanied by an adult. Bring the eggs home in a bottle and observe how they develop into adult frogs.

3 What other animals moult? Look around the house or in gardens near your home. See if you can find moults of insects or other animals.

Life Cycles of Plants

You have looked at the life cycles of animals so far. What about plants? What are their life cycles like?

In Joe and Sue's garden...

Most plants grow from seeds. Let's observe the life cycle of the tomato plant.

Seeds of the tomato plant

Life Cycle of the Tomato Plant

A seed needs air, water and warmth before it can **germinate** or start to grow.

a few days later...

The root grows first.

root

Soon, the shoot appears.

shoot

A young plant is called a **seedling**. At first, the seedling gets its food from the seed. When leaves develop, the seedling starts making its own food.

17

As the seedling grows, more leaves develop to help make food. More roots grow to help the plant take in water and mineral salts from the soil.

After several weeks, flowers appear on the plant.

The flowers develop into small tomato fruits. The small fruits grow bigger and turn from green to red. This is the time to pick the tomatoes and make a nice dish with them!

You can use the seeds of the tomatoes to grow more tomato plants. In this way, you will have a never-ending supply of tomatoes!

Like the tomato plant, any plant grown from a seed passes through these stages in its life cycle:

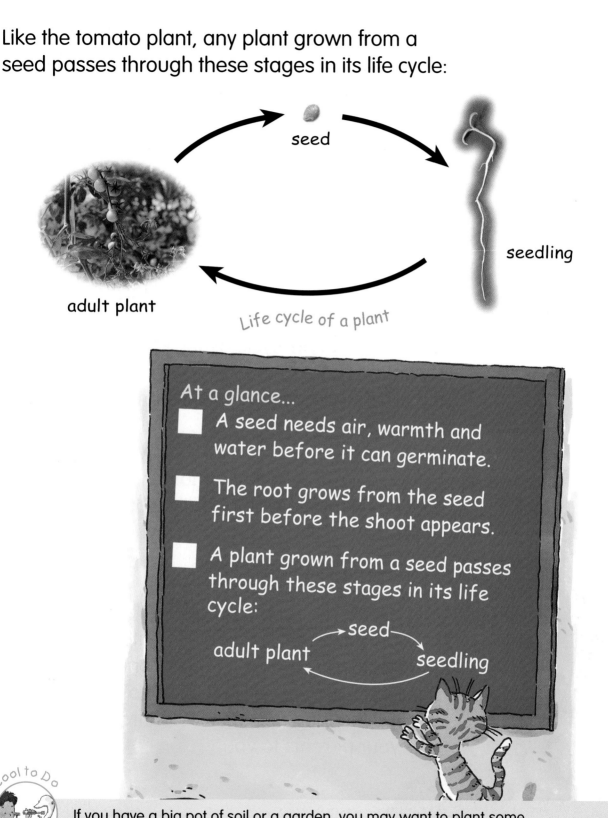

seed

seedling

adult plant

Life cycle of a plant

At a glance...

☐ A seed needs air, warmth and water before it can germinate.

☐ The root grows from the seed first before the shoot appears.

☐ A plant grown from a seed passes through these stages in its life cycle:

adult plant → seed → seedling

Cool to Do

If you have a big pot of soil or a garden, you may want to plant some groundnuts and watch them grow. If you are lucky, you may be able to get fruits after about three months.

19

Pass it On

Whether they are animals or plants, living things always reproduce their own kind. Cats will always give birth to kittens, and bean plants will always produce seeds that will grow into young bean plants. The young will have a similar life cycle as their parents. This repeating pattern makes sure that there will always be living things of the same kind around.

Look at a picture of yourself with your parents. Do you look more like your father or mother? Which of your features look like your father? Which of your features look like your mother?

Try rolling your tongue into a U shape.

Can you do it? Ask your parents to try rolling their tongues too. If you can, one of your parents should be able to do so! This ability to roll the tongue is passed on from one of your parents to you.

Some other characteristics that may be passed on from the parent to the child are height, colour of the hair, colour and size of the eyes, and shape of the ears. Because characteristics are passed on, living things always look like their parents.

This is true of you. It is true of all living things.

In the case of a butterfly, the adult takes after its parents even though the young does not.

Who are our parents?

At a glance...
- ☐ Characteristics of parents can be passed on to their young.
- ☐ Living things closely resemble their parents.

Systems

A system is made up of parts. These parts work together to carry out a certain job. Every part is important. If one part of the system is missing or not working right, the system cannot carry out its job properly.

A system can be something simple. A pencil is a system. It is made up of a few parts — the wooden outer layer, the lead inside and the eraser at the top. Each part helps in its own special way in the task of writing. Do you know what each part is for?

A system can also be something complex. A computer is a complex system. It is made up of many parts.

These form a computer system.

A living thing is a very complex system. Each animal or plant is made up of many smaller systems. These systems help the living thing to carry out important jobs such as breathing and growing. Each of these systems are made up of many parts.

Each part of a system does a job that is different from the rest. Together, they make sure that the system works properly.

A Living Thing as a System

Every living thing, whether it is an animal or a plant, is a system. A living thing is made up of many parts. Each part does a special job. All the parts work together to keep the living thing alive and healthy.

Parts of Animals

Animals have parts known as organs. These organs help to meet the needs of the animals. Examples of organs are the eyes, ears and nose.

An eagle has sharp eyes. The eyes help it to spot a rat far away so that it can catch the rat for food.

A bat's good sense of hearing helps it to find its way about in the dark.

A mole has lots of tiny hairs on its nose that are sensitive to movement. These help the mole to move around in dark tunnels.

The Senses of Taste and Smell

Your tongue helps you to taste. It is covered with thousands of tiny taste buds. Different groups of taste buds pick out different types of taste. That is how you know when food is sweet, sour, bitter or salty.

Bits 'n' Bites

Can you imagine tasting food with your feet? Insects such as flies and butterflies taste with the bottom of their feet. This allows them to know if what they are standing on is worth eating!

Your nose can detect different smells.

Bits 'n' Bites

Dogs have a very good sense of smell. Their sense of smell is at least 40 times better than yours. They can find things just by following the smell that is left behind by something or someone. This is why dogs are often used to find missing people.

Smells are carried by tiny particles that float in the air. When you breathe, these tiny particles go into your nose. Your nose sends a message to your brain. You can then tell what you are smelling.

How is your sense of smell useful to you? Being able to smell can warn you of danger. It can tell you if something is burning, or if you are eating rotten food that will make you ill.

Partners at work

Bits 'n' Bites

Your sense of smell is much more sensitive than your sense of taste. Your tongue knows four tastes. Your nose knows about 3000 different types of smells.

Joe has a blocked nose. His favourite chicken rice just doesn't taste the same!

All your senses work together, but smell and taste are special partners. When you eat an apple, your nose smells the fruit and your tongue tastes the sweetness. Together, they help you enjoy your apple. When you have a cold, you cannot smell so well. Your food seems to lose some of its flavour.

The Sense of Hearing

Your ear is the sense organ that helps you to hear.

Ding **Dong!**

How are Joe, Sue and their mother using their ears?

The outer ear collects sounds.

The eardrum shakes or vibrates when sounds reach it. The vibrations travel to other parts of the ear and a message is then sent to the brain.

You can tell if sounds are loud or soft, high-pitched or low-pitched, pleasant or unpleasant, familiar or unfamiliar.

Why is the sense of hearing important? What happens if you do not have the use of your sense of hearing?

Bits 'n' Bites

The sound a cow makes is low-pitched. The squeak of a mouse is high-pitched. Some sounds are so high-pitched that the human ear cannot detect them. However, animals such as dolphins, bats and dogs can hear these sounds.

Watch out, Joe!

The Sense of Touch

Your skin is responsible for your sense of touch. It is also the largest organ of your body. You can feel with every part of your skin although your lips and fingertips are especially sensitive. You can tell if something is

smooth or rough,

hot or cold.

You can also tell if something is pressing softly or heavily against your skin.

When something sharp pricks you, you sense pain.

Ouch!

What do you think may happen if you lose your sense of touch?

Together in Action

You make use of your senses of sight, taste, smell, hearing and touch every day, sometimes without you even realising it.

Oooh... what's that bright light! It's so glaring!

It's the morning sun. I'll send a message to your body to get out of bed.

Hmm... sniff, sniff. It smells like ....

It's ham and eggs. I'll send a message to the legs to go into the kitchen to get some.

37

Group & Share

Can you think of activities that make use of two or more sense organs at one time?

At a glance...

■ You have five sense organs. They are the eyes, ears, nose, tongue and skin.

■

Sense organ	Sense
Eyes	Sight
Ears	Hearing
Nose	Smell
Tongue	Taste
Skin	Touch

■ The five senses together help you gather valuable information about the world around you.

In this book, you will study in detail the digestive, skeletal and muscular systems. You will learn more about the other two systems in Primary 4.

At a glance...
- [ ] The body is a complex system.
- [ ] The body is made up of several important systems that work together.

The Digestive System

Sue has just had a delicious breakfast! Do you know what happens to the food after she has swallowed it?

Your body needs food to give it energy to grow and work properly. However, your body cannot use the food you eat just as it is.

Food has to be chewed or chopped up, then changed inside you into simple substances. This process is called **digestion**.

Pizza in its original state cannot be used by the body.

There is a great diversity of things, both living and non-living, around you. These things affect one another. We say that they **interact**.

Interactions

A doorstop interacts with a door to keep it open. A paper clip interacts with sheets of paper to hold them together. Your muscles interact with your bones to help you move.

Living things interact with one another. Some animals eat other animals. They may fight for food or a place to live in. Animals also interact with plants. Animal droppings fertilise the soil so that plants can grow well. In return, plants provide animals with food and shelter.

Living things interact with non-living things. We use machines to help us work more efficiently. We also use vehicles to travel to faraway places. These interactions benefit us.

However, some interactions are harmful to people. For example, cars and other vehicles we drive give out poisonous gases that harm our health.

Can you name some interactions which benefit us and some which cause us harm?

When the ends of the wire are connected to a battery, the iron nail becomes a magnet. Test your electromagnet to see if it picks up the same things as your ordinary bar magnet.

The electromagnet is only a magnet when electricity is flowing through the wires. Once electricity stops flowing, the iron nail becomes an ordinary nail again. It is no longer a magnet and does not attract magnetic objects.

Group & Share

Discuss with your friend ways to make an electromagnet stronger.

Bits 'n' Bites

A steel nail used as an electromagnet is able to retain its magnetism for some time even after electricity stops flowing in the wires.

Never try using electricity from the mains to make an electromagnet. This is far too dangerous and could kill you.

80

At a glance...

☐ A magnetic object can be magnetised by stroking it many times in the same direction with a magnet.

☐ A non-magnetic object cannot be magnetised.

☐ An electromagnet can be made by coiling an electrical wire round a magnetic object many times, and connecting the ends of the wire to a battery.

Cool to Do

Make a list of objects that can be magnetised, and another that cannot. Find out why only magnetic objects can be turned into magnets.

Magnets, Magnets, Everywhere

When most people think of magnets, they picture in their minds a bar magnet or a horseshoe magnet. However, magnets can come in many other forms. You are probably making use of magnets every day without even realising it.

Daily Uses of Magnets

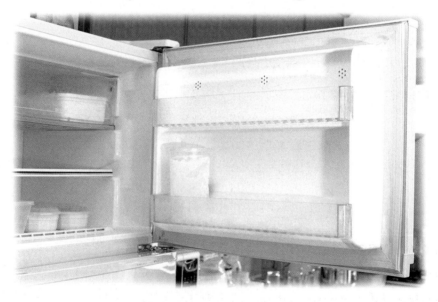

A magnet keeps the door of a refrigerator shut. A thin long magnet is hidden inside a rubber strip around the refrigerator door. A refrigerator is made of steel, so the magnet allows the door to be tightly shut when you close it.

Some pencil boxes remain shut with the help of magnets. Does your pencil box contain a magnet too?

steel piece

magnet

button magnet

Some ladies' handbags have magnets that keep the handbags closed. This ensures that the belongings inside do not fall out easily.

Some doorstops keep doors open by making use of magnetic attraction. A magnet in the doorstop attracts a piece of iron or steel that is fixed on the door.

Magnets are also used to hold messages on refrigerators or magnetic noticeboards. The attraction of a magnet works through non-magnetic materials such as paper. Hence the magnet can hold the paper in place by attracting the magnetic object behind it.

MEMO

Mum,
CCA after
school. Will
be back home
late!

Many household appliances such as vacuum cleaners, radios and washing machines also have magnets in them.

Other Uses of Magnets and Magnetic Materials

Magnets are used in compasses to show directions as they always rest in the North-South direction. Compasses are especially important to hikers, soldiers and sailors. Which part of the compass is a magnet? Why do you think so?

needle

casing

compass

Very strong electromagnets are used to separate iron and steel objects from other things which are thrown away. The iron and steel can be used again to make other things.

A computer uses magnets to display images on a screen. Computer floppy disks also store information with the help of magnetic material.

Cassette and video tapes contain magnetic tapes that can store sound and pictures.

Use a magnet to stroke an old, unwanted cassette tape. Try playing the tape after that. The tape will not work properly because your magnet has destroyed the information recorded in the tape.

Bits 'n' Bites

Your Mass Rapid Transit (MRT) farecard contains a magnetic strip. This strip helps to store information such as the value left in your card and even the time you enter an MRT station. Keep your MRT card away from magnets!

Look at the picture showing Joe's home. Can you tell which things have magnets in them?

Look at my home!

At a glance...

☐ Magnets are used to hold objects together.

☐ Many electrical appliances need magnets to work.

☐ Magnets are used in compasses to show directions.

☐ Magnets are used to lift heavy objects made of iron and steel, and to separate them from other things that are thrown away.

Cool to Do

1   Make a list of all the uses of magnets you can think of. You may look up reference books at the library to increase your list.

2   Imagine that you are a scientist. Invent a device that makes use of a magnet to carry out a job. Try building this device.